THE GUCCI BAG

ALSO BY IRVING LAYTON

Here and Now   1945
Now Is the Place   1948
The Black Huntsmen   1951
Cerberus (with Louis Dudek & Raymond Souster)   1952
Love the Conqueror Worm   1953
In the Midst of My Fever   1954
The Long Pea-Shooter   1954
The Blue Propeller   1955
The Cold Green Element   1955
Music on a Kazoo   1956
The Bull Calf and Other Poems   1956
The Improved Binoculars   1956
A Laughter in the Mind   1958
A Red Carpet for the Sun   1959
The Swinging Flesh (Poems and Stories)   1961
Balls For a One-Armed Juggler   1963
The Laughing Rooster   1964
Collected Poems   1965
Periods of the Moon   1967
The Shattered Plinths   1968
Selected Poems   1969
The Whole Bloody Bird   1969
Nail Polish   1971
The Collected Poems of Irving Layton   1971
Engagements: Prose of Irving Layton   1972
Lovers and Lesser Men   1973
Seventy-Five Greek Poems   1974
The Pole-Vaulter   1974
The Darkening Fire   1975
The Unwavering Eye   1975
For My Brother Jesus   1976
Taking Sides   1977
The Covenant   1977
The Poems of Irving Layton   1977
The Uncollected Poems of Irving Layton   1977
The Tightrope Dancer   1978
Droppings from Heaven   1979
An Unlikely Affair   1980
For My Neighbours in Hell   1980
The Love Poems of Irving Layton   1980
Europe and Other Bad News   1981
A Wild Peculiar Joy   1982
The Gucci Bag   (Mosaic Press, Limited Edition)   1983
The Gucci Bag   1983

The Gucci Bag
Irving Layton

McCLELLAND AND STEWART

The Canadian Publishers
McClelland and Stewart Limited
25 Hollinger Road, Toronto M4B 3G2

Canadian Cataloguing in Publication Data

Layton, Irving, 1912–
   The Gucci bag

Poems.
Contents vary from Mosaic Press ed., 1983.

ISBN 0-7710-4917-X

I. Title.

PS8523.A98G83 1983   C811'.54   C83-098768-1
PR9199.3.L39G83 1983

The publisher makes grateful acknowledgment to the Ontario Arts Council for its assistance.

Set in Trump Mediaeval by The Typeworks, Vancouver
Printed and bound in Canada

FOR GYPSY JO

A wonderful flower child
I used to know

Mankind divides unfairly into the divine and the bovine.

There's indeed one law for the rich and the poor, but only the rich can afford it.

I want to go into the sunset with both pitchforks blazing.

FOREWORD

ALL THAT I KNOW ABOUT JACK THE RIPPER CAN BE PUT INTO A SMALL thimble. The encyclopedias appear to be no more knowledgeable on the subject than I. They merely tell us that he was a pseudonymous murderer who slashed the throats of at least seven women, all prostitutes, in London's East End from August 7 to November 10, 1888. The failure to arrest the killer forced the resignation of the police commissioner and the home secretary. There has been speculation that the Ripper's identity was known to the police but because there was more than a drop of royal blood coursing through his veins their hands were tied.

There are elements in the life and career of England's most famous murderer that make him a very suggestive symbol for the times in which we are presently living. To put the matter quickly and bluntly: the times are murderous and each day grow more so. The facts to warrant this assertion being sufficiently well-known, it's unnecessary to expatiate on them at any great length. Death might cut down any one of us: in a bar by some killer who takes it into his demented head to shoot up the place, or by an arsonist wishing to warm the cockles of his heart by seeing human beings running out of a building sheathed in flames. We can leave out the terrorism which has spread like a plague around the world or the furious preparations for war every country is making in what may turn out to be mankind's last dance of death. Both underline the general insanity that seems to have gripped the inhabitants of this singular planet.

For me Jack the Ripper is a metaphor for the technological and commercial world that was first written into the annals of history by the European bourgeoisie that went on from there to embroider the script with two world wars, the vicious depredations of colonialism, the spread of bourgeois-Christendom to every corner of the globe, the smoking chimneys of Auschwitz and Belsen, the murderous insanities of Leninism. From my own perspective the last-named is not a dialectical contradiction to capitalism but rather the unfettered development of its very core and rationale, the profit motive. What, after all, is more profitable in our time than human wretchedness? As a commodity, everyone traffics in it since its dividends are greater and more certain than those which even the best securities can be expected to yield. In our bourgeois-bolshevik era anyone who can grab himself a corner in human flesh, in human misery, has been certain of making a killing. Balzac, Flaubert, and Zola chronicled for their readers the avarice, philistinism and heartlessness of the French bourgeoisie. A host of talented Russian poets and novelists have done an even more convincing job of relating to readers, those still capable of being horrified by the evidence of human malevolency, the unspeakable infamies that Lenin and his most vicious disciple, Stalin, loosed upon the world. Foremost among those writers, one must place that extraordinary genius, Solzhenitsyn.

I have one other reason for thinking of Jack the Ripper as metaphor and symbol. He was undoubtedly the product of nearly two thousand years of Christianity and its deep anti-sexual psychosis. I can't imagine anyone like him appearing in the pagan, pre-Christian world. Undoubtedly St. Paul and the church fathers and after them the Calvinists and Methodists had a big hand in his making. If I were doing a painting of Jack the Ripper slashing the throat of one of his victims I'd have him doing it with a crucifix. The spread of sexual repressiveness to whatever part of the world it was able to get a foothold in is certainly one of the more gruesome crimes that Christianity has on its conscience. The other one is the promulgation and spread of antisemitism to wherever the glad tidings of my brother Jesus could be brought. The glad tidings turned out to be KILL JEWS, BURN JEWS, GAS JEWS. Though historians and theologians have by now made Christianity's responsibility for the Holocaust a commonplace, the signs are still wanting of any deep stirrings of conscience among the supposed followers of Christ. I've given up the hope that there ever will be, human nature being what it is. Perhaps I should avoid a possible misunderstanding that might arise at this point and say flatly that I don't think Jack the Ripper was an antisemite. Mind you, if I had to hazard a guess I'd say he probably was, since antisemitism and antieroticism have a common root in the flight from woman, i.e. the fear of life.

I'd like to clear up a likely misunderstanding – the use of the word "Idd" that figures in several of my poems. I am, of course, aware of the pejorative associations that surround the rhyming word that it calls to mind. Many times I heard both my father and mother derisively called "Yid." None of my siblings escaped the appellation in the French-Canadian section of the city where we lived. Nor indeed did I. But I have my reasons for coining the word "Idd." In my foreword to *The Covenant*, I distinguished between Christians and Xians, the latter being conventional churchgoers who have no intention of ever putting into practice any of the moral precepts which Jesus preached for their salvation and in whose name – tragic historical paradox – antisemitism was preached to more than half the globe. It should never be forgotten that it was Xians, eager hordes of them, who did their utmost to bring about the extermination of the six million Jews who lived in their midst.

But if the distinction between Christians and Xians is apposite, so is the one between Jews and Idds. Idds and Xians have this much in common: they both pay lip-service to religious intuitions given to them by Hebrew prophets. I use philistine, babbitt, materialist, Idd, as interchangeable terms. The Idd is also a bigot: he thinks *moneytheism* is the one true faith. However, very much in his favour is that he knows better. The tablets which Moses brought down from Mount Sinai have given him a moral migraine from which he vainly seeks relief. I therefore define an Idd as a mercenary oaf with a conscience. It's a useful term that I hope will replace the evil caricature of the Jew that has been in circulation until now. Idds are tragi-comic figures that plead for compassion and understanding. But, should anyone think I've written too harshly about Idds, he might turn to what the poet-prophets, Amos and Jeremiah, had to say about their swaggering counterparts in ancient Judea.

What makes for enduring poetry is the intersection between the personal and the universal: on a lesser scale, between the personal and social. Only a handful of North American poets have essayed anything like that in recent decades. Robert Lowell? John Berryman? Who else? Is there a poet anywhere in Canada or in the United States who is addressing himself with the full force of his talent and personality to the inequities and insanities which our viciously insane world is manifesting on all sides? The professors and critics, as I predicted in numerous prefaces, have done their deadly work. More at home with ideas and abstractions than they are with feelings and experiences, their influence has been such as to practically eliminate personality from contemporary poetry. It's almost impossible in the welter of anonymous voices to distinguish one poetaster from another. Such puny, timorous, crepitant voices. Wherever Pushkin, Byron, Rimbaud, Whitman, and Lawrence are, they must be having a tremendous laugh – if they're not sorrowing over the fabrication of poems that are so completely lacking in individual mood, flavour, and substance that one surmises their authors have surreptitiously made use of computers.

There's also the mindlessness of surrealistic verse that reads as if it had been composed by computers recovering from an alcoholic binge. Still, if vibrators are now in general use for giving their possessors multiple orgasms, why shouldn't mechanical devices of one sort or another be used to compose poems? Especially since very few nowadays care about their composition one way or another. Even a smaller number know what a poem is supposed to look or feel like, the educational system having junked the study of poetry along with Greek and Latin. As far as the average technological barbarian is concerned, male and female, the three of them are dead languages. Matthew Arnold was surely daydreaming when he asserted that poetry was bound to replace religion as a shaping influence on people's beliefs and conduct. It simply hasn't happened. It's even less likely to happen in Canada where culture is nothing more than dressing on a McDonald's hamburger.

The poet is someone who can't help mythologizing his experiences. He exaggerates, distorts, fictionalizes. In him the will-to-power takes the form of investing even the trifling and banal with symbolic significance. But the poet is also someone who makes lucky things happen, for his life is a destiny or a destination. Symbols? Returning from an annual trip to Europe, some friends handed me the gift they had bought for me – a Gucci bag. Since it was not especially eye-catching and was too small to be useful, I straightaway put it into a drawer where over the passing weeks and months, it collected antshit and a thin layer of dust. After all, what's a restless, grey-haired poet to do with a Gucci bag? Can one imagine Goethe sporting one? Or the much younger and more flamboyant Byron? If, as I believe, the poet's journey is towards self-definition, Gucci bags are an unnecessary encumbrance. Certainly the poet's journey will take him on many side trips, some of them harrowing enough to put welts on his soul that will never go away. And that's as it must and should be, for his task always is to alchemize the "crude" into "essence," into the energizing fuels that others may use to light their way on their no less difficult journey towards that Goodnight and Nothingness that awaits us all.

At present the Gucci bag is nailed to my outside housewall to keep away the vampires of materialism and acquisitiveness. A talisman, it also serves as a constant reminder of how easy it is to slide into the Inferno of lovelessness, pride and greed, and of the bloated soulless faces one encounters there. Every poet discovers – uncovers – his own hell. Is perhaps inevitably constrained to make it. Mine is the bourgeois world with its contempt for the claims of beauty, justice, truth, and compassion.

So it's to the murderous stealth of Jack the Ripper, brutally snuffing out life, that I must finally come back. The feeling persists in me that the life-blood of poetry is slowly draining away. Poetry is the most intense and meaningful articulation of human experience. That articulation has grown feebler and feebler as this century wears on. Does it indicate the exhaustion of our narcissistic bourgeois-bolshevist culture with its stress on material possessions, its encouragement of those two impulses, fear and greed, which Brooks Adams saw as the dominant factors in the rise and decay of civilizations? It seems doubtful to me that poetry, soaring on its pinions of exuberance and creativeness, can continue to flourish in the miasma of a depersonalizing culture. The atmosphere will not long sustain it. Too many somnambulistic cripples whom technology, and the dulling routines it enforces, have squeezed dry of feeling and imagination. Too many half-men and half-women! Like the exposed and vulnerable prostitutes Jack the Ripper killed, poetry exists to give relief to those dark sensual impulses that our over-mechanized civilization has all but snuffed out. If that's how I read the handwriting on the wall, who will blame me if on certain brooding nights I see his bloodstained knife raised for the final slash?

I

There's a crack
in the soul of every man
 and woman
that opens up to betrayal and worse.
Just a small hairline crack
 and the devil walks in.

So I've nailed a Gucci bag
on my outside housewall
 where in plain sight
it hangs like a Transylvanian bat
to dismay the vampires of possessiveness
 and scare them away.

Daily its fraying look
as it sways in the wind
 calls to mind
evil is not external but within;
the flaw always our own that asks in
 temptation, frailty, and sin.

2

I walked out of my ghetto
into the sweet meadows of your embrace.
I commanded sunlight for the hour.
Like a codicil I read your face.

Many blisses it promised me.
Greek goddesses I saw move
out of your dark eyes and called them
Ecstasy and Freedom and Love.

From our most rapturous sighs
we sowed gardens, we builded a house;
the chandeliers danced on air
when they heard our infant's cry.

The morning teas made us giddier
than the best French champagne.
We lookt into each other's eyes
and kissed and lookt again.

We might have died from an excess
of so much happiness
but a faery who dwells in the Black Forest
divined the peril in our bliss.

She pointed her magical stick
at my head and turned it to old snow.
I still adore your brooding eyes, Love,
but where did the goddesses go?

3

With you gone
I embrace pain,
pleasure's indisseverable twin

I would not unpartner them
even if I could

And I can't
         with you gone
and I, in our bed,
alone

4

"Do not look back
upon the lady when you lead her up from Hell:
disobey, she'll vanish into air, become invisible.

"Never again will you behold her face or form."

I was that singer who heard the gods and obeyed.
I charmed my lady out of Old Forest Hill
where her mother's baubles glittered like devils' eyes.

Not even her father's condo in Palm Beach could keep
that lovely shade.

She was all mine, following me with a bold surmise
from slagheap to slagheap as I played my reed.
I heard her light tread directly behind my own.

Though her nearness bewitched me, I did not turn my head.

O but I longed to see her dear face
more beautiful, perhaps paler, than the asphodel;
to fall on my knees and kiss the folds of her dress.

To take into my lungs once more her fragrant smell.

At last looms before me the grim portal white with dawn.
My foot touches the earth beloved of living men.
I turn eagerly to embrace my love. She is gone.

At the mouth of Hell, once more I stand bereft, alone.

Though I had held the gods above the woman I prized and
        burned for,

the promised guerdon, a woman's love, was not mine.
Here nothing is certain and chance or accident rule
    everything.

Now, more fiercely than ever do I pluck my lyre and sing.

5

Once a seed, now a tree crowned with leaves
that soil and sun, a principium of individuation,
shaped to hang for a summer and then fall.

Stars moulder and rot at a slower rate
or blaze suddenly into blackness
only to bud again on God's unfolding arm.

So my love was a quick seed
whose soil was your smile, its sun your joy.
A sudden frost turned its leaves black.

Black as the black night at my window.
No star will return to pierce the darkness.
No leaf ever bud on my withering stalk.

6

A failed love has disordered my sight.
I look at things with eyes that blight.
Tree, why do you drop leaves that are dead?
Hand me my captived princess instead.

I have garlands for her, joyous poems;
stars and flowers she has never seen.
I shall remodel the earth for her,
find her transports she has never known.

Once the world was a fairy tale
whose leaves the soft wind turned for her;
her smiles were white birchtrees
and each fair rose her remembrancer.

I have journeyed to set my princess free.
Her jewels are light-filled raindrops
on wet boughs that are her arms.
In every sough her voice is calling me.

The ugly witch who changed her limbs
deceived me with her ravishing shape.
Love only was my talisman.
Three times I made my death-defying leap.

Love, great love, has brought me here.
The invidious hag has died of grief
and the hour comes near when my princess
must drop her garment of knotted bole and leaf.

Midday when the warm sun brightly
scatters gloom from the human face
the redeemed lovers shall embrace,
white butterflies dance like the foam-flecked sea.

7

After the great man's reading at Harbourfront
they walked the quieted streets
where warehouses and condominiums
suddenly parcelled out the night for them.

The stars glittered in the sky.
Did they or the introspective trees they passed
hear him say: "Leave me, I'm a man possessed.
My fury and wisdom are not for your lenient pulse"?

What purpose in reason or foreknowledge when love
bends the will as if it were wet straw?
When appetite, hardening the member, makes butter
of the mind? His being sagged in her embrace.

The incoherent words the stars made him speak
punctuated the darkness like the streetlamps
that moved towards them: prehistoric giants
holding torches high above their heads.

Folly or fate now tipped his words with flame.
His own mouth became the foundry for bolts
that rivetted him fast to inexpugnable shame.
Heavy with them he sank at last into the widening swamp.

8

Into the ordinary day you came,
giving your small nose and chin to the air
and blinded by the noise you could not see.
  Your mother's smile was your benediction;
my wonderment will accompany you
all your days. Dear little girl, what blessings
shall I ask for you? Strong limbs, a mind firm
that looking on this world without dismay
turns furious lust into love's romance?
  These, my child, and more. Grace keep you
queenly and kind, a comfort to the ill and poor,
your presence a bounty of joy to all
that have vision of you, as I have now
who hold your fingers in my trembling hand.

9

How can I my Imagination save?
A wondrous child I have and do not have.
The lively blood in me grows slack and chilled.
The cistern is empty that once was filled.

She was the fruit of luxuriant love
and brought me the light from the sun above.
In gorgeous truth she turned each day to spring.
Taken from me, drear is the song I sing.

The Hebrew seer cursed the day he was born.
I too preach to deaf ears, contemned, forlorn.
Inspiration is not for common clay.
Men toil at rooting it out night and day.

My grief is an immense water-logged bowl.
Into it I plunge my frantic soul
to temper it like a spike in clouds of steam.
Now only of foul knife-deaths do I dream.

10

Into the clean air
of a mountainside
I expelled from my lungs
my immoderate scorn
for human baseness.

The next afternoon
on the exact spot
where I had stood,
a tall pinetree had sprung up,
its sharp needles glittering in the sun.

I pierced my skin with one
and drew a wrinkle of blood.
The relief still feels good,
and there are enough of them
to last me a lifetime.

II

He waits in the lawyer's office
till nature compels; then he runs
to ask of the white urinals:
"Has love been distilled into piss?"

Where are the rapt sighings in bed?
The passionate kisses and bites?
The gracious perfumes that fed him
fuel for his exuberant flights?

When he soared above the city
with metaphors and tropes for wings
and wrote into the clear blue sky
"Thrice blessed is the lover who sings."

More joyous than Shelley's skylark
he was; more arrogant than the hawk
who now is besieged by lawyers
and by urinal bubbles mocked.

12

That WASP Toronto lawyer
walks like a man,
even from time to time
smiles and talks like one.

But look more carefully,
appearance
can deceive.

He's really
(do you see it now?)
an immaculately dressed
dung beetle.

Revelling
in everyone's bourgeois shit
and straining . . . straining hard
to leave his rank name
lying on top of it.

13

Stranger, keep your six-shooter handy;
the only justice you'll ever see
comes smoking out of its barrels.

In Gulch Valley,
the sheriff's always stoned;
anyway, in the furlined pocket
of Joe Mucho, the saloon-keeper.

Though justice haunts the fevered brains
of prophets and poets, teases
like a half-remembered dream,
in the real world of rustlers
and flap-ear'd knaves
it swings to the ring of their silver dollars.

The citizens? Bah.
They're too scared to do anything
about their notions of right and wrong.
They'll moan and groan and wish
the killings don't take too long
so they can go back to feeling
decent honourable folk again.

Only the Lone Ranger's footfall
makes the corrupt judge shudder,
gives him bad dreams.

Poems are his silver bullets:
sizzling quatrains, a burst of couplets.

When he shoots them into the air
to scatter the massing shadows,

they drop from the clouds
on varmint and huckster,
chilling them into a still life forever.

Niagara-on-the Lake
August 1, 1982

14

At the height of their bitter quarrel
the wretched woman taunted him:
"Poetry is one thing, life another."

And indeed she was right to do so,
for her brief days will soon be over
but she will live infamous in his poems forever.

15

A body that's dead decays and rots.
Flies gather when it begins to stink
and sages smell no sweeter than sots.
Give heed, peasants, it's later than you think.

For yearning to save a woman's soul
daily he read her some living verse;
but for her the sun and moon were dead
and all that magic was powerless.

A decaying body reeks to heaven
but souls that corrupt smell worse, far worse.
A dead soul takes sweetness from the air,
on life itself lays down its black curse.

He's neither green dragon nor red;
he has lost his connection with the sun.
His lady's soul is dying, is dead,
and there's none can save her now, no one.

16

For the great wrong she had done me
my mouth had framed a curse
but I did not give it utterance.

For I saw she was under sentence
to feel her soul dying piecemeal,
her frame becoming its shroud and hearse.

17

I lie on my hotel bed
and watch the clouds move across the sky;
they are in no hurry, they move slowly,
but they never pause or rest,
They are light and have their place
   in the universe
When I close my eyes I can imagine
I have been dreaming of sheep.
The days also pass slowly.
They too are light and have their place.
I swim, converse with a friend, read poetry.
   Everything passes, even a woman's malice
when she knows she is no longer loved,
and her body, no longer desired, is only
a heavy insupportable weight to be coddled
   and dragged from room to room,
its orifices useless.
But that woman too has her place in the universe
   and moves relentlessly on.

18

for S. Ross

Solitary
as that lightning-blasted birch
I take comfort from leaves
falling

They tell me nothing
                              endures forever
neither civilizations
nor a woman's malice

Denuding the thicket
leaf by leaf
decay and the punishing minutes
this day
gladden my heart with promise

Only from rot
are new shining worlds begot

19

The long dark September nights are come,
reminding the vacant poet of losses;
there are no stars in his skull,
only blackness, the fumes of dead loves.

Jerusalem is ruined and pillaged
and her kings and queens are grimacing marionettes.
Where is majesty? Beauty? The courtesies of love?
The stiffening valour in sinew and thigh?

They lie unnoticed on his kitchen floor:
broken pieces of wood, the colours dissolving
into echoes a rising wind amplifies
to a pitch his wearied heart no longer hears.

After each night's solitary meal
he plays blind man's bluff with shadows
that recite lines from his own poems
to mock him as he reaches out hands to touch.

Old poets know that game well.
Designs of soft vulvas cover the walls. Only when
he removes the tight blindfold from his eyes
will a fleshless mouth kiss him with his own passion.

20

When hourly I praised her perfect mouth
How could I have known, with lust besotted,
That Satan himself had forged those red lips
To singe my wings, to crisp me like a moth?

2I

Light on leaves. For me
the most glorious sight earth has to offer.
Greedily I eat, stuffing each bright glitter
into my eyes, always hungering for more.
Who can despair or be unhappy
because he's not seven feet tall
or published in twenty-three languages?

The kitchen's bereft of table and chairs;
white question marks, the cupboard door handles
importune the silence when the radio
stops playing Chopin's sonatas.
The notes lisp and lapse on the stripped walls.

I am alone with my madness and pain.
No voice comes from any part of the house
and all the mirrors in it
are waiting for me to rise from the chair
and release my reflections, one after another,
as I pass from room to empty room.

Nothing is as it was one year ago.
Only the light on twig and leaf is unchanged,
Heraclitus and his flux be damned!
Beauty's radiance is eternal, perfect;
sunlight on leaf will still be here
after I'm gone and taken all my angers with me.
Another bewildered mortal sit
where I am sitting now, perhaps to dream
of the perfect murder, unsolvable as the mystery of creation,
the killer being none other than Oscar Wilde
or the Count of Monte Cristo
come back for his revenges.

22

A malicious, potbellied, arthritic Jew
sees my head trembling slightly.

A bright hope lights up his eyes
and his smile is one
of pure innocent satisfaction
 – it might be Parkinson's disease!

I try to imagine the intense joy
leukemia or a paralyzing stroke
would give him.

When a simple neck exercise
clears up the trouble
the scowl on his face, in turn,
makes me rejoice for days.

In this fashion
do the Chosen People
obey the Mosaic injunction
to make glad their neighbour's heart.

23

Circe lives and performs her ancient ill.
Those lusting for gold she turns into swine.
Lead me out of their dark and fetid hell.
Let your grace and dissembling smile be mine.

24

Not to gloat or boast
as you fry your enemy
to a black toast.

Not to spit
in his staring eye
as you watch him die.

Not to be sad
that his agony gratifies
and makes you humanly glad.

But at the end
to give him decent burial
and send him back to hell.

25

Foolish man, why should I curse your breath
since like myself you're marked out for death?
When our arthritic joints loosen and rot
who will care then who was seer and who sot?

26

My flatted hand descends.
It's too late for him to write his will
or think about estranged wife and friends. Best
just to lie still and keep hoping he'll be able
to hobble to his notary
                              when what's happened's
all over. For now he must
wait till complete awareness returns
and lie, as now, unmoving and quiet
since not yet undazed enough to crawl
to where the smells of mowed grass
are coming from
                              or the fine points
of fractured light.

He begins a faint buzz, a feeble stir
                                          spins
himself around, once, once more,
like a minuscule coin or turnstile
a hand has twirled into motion
                              stops all of a sudden
to get his bearings and rest. Another buzz
this time much louder
                              marking out a silence
in which to consider possible meanings.

Was it another insect, larger, more powerful?
The wind that
                  when the luck's with him
usually lifts his wings
and escorts him from hedge to hedge?
Perhaps a Fly-God he'd ignorantly overlooked
or hadn't sufficiently flattered or propitiated?

Or, as now seems most likely,
the ledge he was hopping towards when he felt
the sharp thunder at his back
                              and everything
went suddenly inexplicably black?

27

I'd like to be a humanist
but humans
             won't let me.
They rise up at extraordinary moments
to spoil my plans
                  for moulding myself
into Erasmus or Montaigne.
Y'know what I mean: benevolence shining
in both blue eyes, spouting
humanist sentiments in daily and/or
weekly bulletins.

Take Idds for instance.
I've a long acquaintance
                        with them
going back (for a start) to my
brothers-in-law
               two of them
loudmouthed, moneymad, sadistic bastards,
the third
         a religious sot.

My father was not an Idd
                         he was a Jew.
A gentle visionary too good for this world.
Nobody ever asked him for his signature.
His word was good enough.
                          Where
do you find his sort of integrity nowadays?
Of one of his sons-in-law he said:
"If you'd spit on his face
he'd say it was raining."

I've been barbecued by hardworking Idds

many times, by gentiles
                    seldom or never.
There must be a moral in that somewhere.
If my father were alive he'd tell me;
as it is, he looks down
from his place in heaven
                    and sighs.

And now I read (c.j.n. July 27, 1981)
that camps are going kosher
right across Ontario.
After Spinoza and Marx, Freud and Einstein,
back to respectable middle-class pieties,
back to the rabbis twirling their forelocks,
their bad breath and hypocrisy.
Ain't that something to cheer about?
Kashruth in Canada
and Begin's bombers bringing peace
to the cadavers in Lebanon.

Bah. To cheer myself
I'll read Jeremiah again
and Ecclesiastes.
                    If these fail
there's always Job to fall back on.

28

In unrepressed anger because
she chose wealth before her daimon
the wretched woman made a furrow
in my cottage windowscreen.

I shall keep it so, unmended.
It reminds me of her mouth, always
open and twisted with self-loathing.
But wordless, mere wire, it says nothing.

29

Does the Jew need a state or army?
Remembering the injunction: "Lo, he dwells alone
and shall not be numbered among the nations"
let him dismiss at once the diplomats
and bankers, the wealthy swindlers and jurists,
the career officers and munition-makers.
Let him hang proud and independent
from God's armpit. How did it happen
the noisome Idd usurps his place to become
a universal scandal and reproach? What
malignity put him at the head of governments,
insurance companies and corporations?
In hot pursuit of power and success are not
the affluent moneytheists of Old Forest Hill
an evil deformity, the Israelites' shed skin?
Their stylish wives and daughters ogling
the latest shipment of baubles in Miami and Tel Aviv,
lice in the beards of Moses and the prophets?
Who today speaks for that singular remnant
and the desert revelation it gospelled from Moses
to Jesus: love and creativity, freedom from oppression?
I hear only cannons speak, the loudly stuttering Uzzi.
I hear the cries of well-padded martial Idds
in their exclusive clubs and synagogues;
the piteous sigh of the Holocaust Jew
bewailing his ashes, the pious snarl of the bigot.
But that other voice, the voice exhorting them
to stand alone and be a light to the gentiles
is not heard. O who will dissolve
the terrible silence into bread and wine?

30

Once they talked to God

Afterwards they harangued mankind

For a time they buttonholed its poets
and visionaries, the righteous in all lands

Now, in their plush synagogues
they are talking only to themselves

31

All is vanity, so it's writ
and life's a lump of brown shit.

Carve thou a noble name on it.

32

O Israel, where are your poets?
Your prophets and visionaries?
Your marvellous storytellers with their
terrible tales of right and wrong?
Your dreamers and makers of song?
They are all gone and will come no more.
Others plead the cause of the weak and poor.
Others contemn injustice and war.
Where, my people, is that fine delirium
about love and the millennium?

The sleek businessman usurps their place.
the executive with clean-shaved face
and smooth flexible tongue
that mommicks right and wrong.
When I look across the land I see
the suave rabbi and pharisee.
Passion and anger are not theirs;
in the marketplace they sell other wares:
gilt-edged bonds, a building site;
their honour if the bribe is right.

Snug in his downtown office
Isaiah is too ambitious to remind us
a people without vision perishes.
Jeremiah is taking important calls
and has no time to speak of idols.
Amos is a middle-class socialist,
the Preacher a suburban hedonist.
Once, ah, once it was different.
God his messages through his prophets sent.
But that was long, long ago
and I eat the exile's bread of sorrow.

33

He created as warblers sing,
as butterflies mate on white fences.

Delight was his, natural as grass,
as the lovely scents of flowers and logs
after rain. What can vindicate creation
so much as an old delirious man
in love with his life and wife,
the words coming at the right time
to the right beat?

He saw drunks dozing on park benches
or stretched out on sidewalks, asleep.
Happy mortals, he mused, happy, happy mortals,
oblivious of neglect and humiliation,
of all that humans
hold in store for other miserable humans;
to abuse, betrayal, insult
and the raging fires of egotism
in which all must finally char.

His was the joy of self-renewing energy
at war with inertness or that activity
that has possessions for its aim
(another kind of death but one that fools
undertakers who go only by smells).
Now, turned out of that green Eden
he celebrated in poem after poem,
he must listen when inspired lawyers
decode his messages to posterity
or debate its finer points with policemen
and the torpid philistines they protect;
finding himself envying the clochards

snoring on the church steps
and learning a new respect for the hardworking
Niçoise whores he remembers guarding
their corner beats against all newcomers.

34

Yesterday I pulled my bobsled
up the highest hill
in our slum neighbourhood

Slow and thick the snowflakes
fell on my head.
I became the wonderworld around me.

I do not remember ever
turning the bobsled around.
What am I doing in that woman's bed?

35

Madman, born to strife as sparks fly upward.
A martyr to rapture and swift revulsion,
woman was the weight you bore, her soft limbs
around your neck, her hands gripping your hair.

Your discarded wives? Ecstasies you suffered
till suffering became your ecstasy,
the healthful dram of poison in your dramas.
You played with marriages as a child with blocks.

Giddyap: Giddyap to the heights. Whipping you
with epiphanies welts alone can yield,
Hecate lashed you on to greatness.
Now men live more sanely for your madness.

Morality's a cloak for neurosis, you raged;
the sinner's delighting reek of guilt
consoles mankind for its fall from grace.
Men must clean their hands in their neighbour's blood.

For life's a cess in woman's lovely crotch
where's sown Christ's crown of spikes and thorns.
Every poet must find his Magdalene
who when he's dead will cry his resurrection.

36

This one entreats a great passion
to give him the courage
of his animality

And that one dreams
of raping a woman,
loathing not her but life
that put ashes in his veins

Nietzsche saw his greatness affirmed
when costermonger women
found the sweetest grapes for him

37

When the white-haired poet in despair
turns away from the mindless noise, from
the twitching figures;
    and apocalyptic images
of well-dressed men feasting on babyflesh
    leap into his head
he thinks happily of the neutron bomb,
his face taking on again
    the proud and serene look
that once brought women in their hundreds
    clamouring to his bed

38

Dear girl, all the women I ever loved
had lovers they wanted to talk about.
Over the years my face
took on the benignity of a priest.

And snow once had the white radiance of a dream,
the air above it sparkling fresh and clean.
I've seen too many sparrows, dead to the world.
If you live long enough, the differences cancel out.

And why do women think their sex life
so fascinating? Or is it disillusion, cold lust,
makes them go on the way they do,
blabbing their silly hearts out?

This life's a cauchemar,
a savage dream from which we never waken.
The roulades of energy are all that matter,
not recollections on a windswept moor.

Ask the malign fates: women adore mass killers
whose members they stiffen to wave
like Mozart's magic flute over the dead,
lying huddled against the cold in fosse and ditch.

39

Alone in my room with one autumnal fly, sleepless,
I make resolutions about love and sacrifice
which the gibbon in my head won't keep
but throws into the typewriter so that a modern composer
will know what they sound like in the brain.
When the orchestra stops playing the unfinished symphony
I rise from my chair to acknowledge the applause.
The dishes, still flirting with the sink,
tell me to insert three resolutions about verse
and soapsuds but the angry gibbon farts them
out of my head. I don't know what to do
about the smoke curling from my mouth and nostrils,
deciding finally to stuff it back into the hot bowl
and start over again. How red the bed coverlets,
hospital white the walls, the face in the mirror
deathly pale from unacted murders. At this hour
dreams become flying knives and bullets,
the corpses all happen in the sequence I propose.
The cosmos stands precisely at 3:12 A.M. as I demolish
the last lawyer, his pleadings so lacking
in grace and dignity I slash his throat
with my unlighted pipe, spilling all its ashes
over his staring eyes and briefs. Any century now
I'll pick myself off the insulated ceiling
and eat the neglected dishes in the wash basin.

40

On the street, just before midnight,
people friendless like myself.
You can tell that by the way they walk:
singly, of course, sometimes partnered by a shadow;
and slowly, slowly, to lengthen the time
it will take before they must retrace their steps
to the empty apartment or bedsitting room
that waits to hear them turn the key in the lock
to be ready for them with its mocking silence.

Some drift into the corner restaurant
to cheer themselves with a jovial pizza,
redolent of shared slicings, companionable quips;
this night the miraculous does not happen
and you see them dislodge an olive or onion ring
with the slow deliberation of a judge giving sentence
or an arthritic woman lifting a fryingpan
in a TV commercial for pain-relieving pills.
Others bolt their food to break free from stupor.

Whether on the street, a moving blur in the dark
that gives a lost piteous blink even to tail-lights,
or inside the harsh-lighted Greasy Spoons
the silent struggle is always for momentum
 – to keep moving – even if it's only forkfuls of pizza
you make disappear into the smaller darkness
of your mouth. For you must depend on such tiny events
as the chomping of your teeth, the flick of your Bic,
to make you feel you're still alive, though in a vacuum.

Toronto
August 17, 1981

41

I was dejected from an old love
when she came to me
with her warm young limbs.
It was an unexpected gift from the gods
who have for their service
the happiness of grey-haired poets;
knowing in their untroubled pavilions
that the ripest wisdom falls
only at the touch of firm breasts
and long rippling thighs.

42

The grass, a green carpet for your loves:
birds, butterflies, gaudy-wing'd insects
you're a brilliant chaos in the clear sunshine.
Neither marriage or other work of man holds you
in January's iced claw but spontaneous, free,
you are all opened parcels of energy.

Bless you, sweet creatures, that come
once more to gossip to me of earth and sun
and the self-scorn in that betrayed soul
who abuses authenticity and truth
in vile conventional service to a woman
– who knows truly a sickness unto death.

Now my heart bounds with you through the air
no less light and frolicsome than you are.
Joyously you sun yourselves and make puns
with sudden dizzying spurts, a surprise
of dips and loops, carollings of motion.
You unscroll Shakespeare's wit before my eyes!

How good it is to be astir on days like this.
Like a man recovered from a long illness
or stern paralysis of nerve and will
finding to his loud delight fingers
can move, arms can stretch or bend, his head
bob and pivot like a playful ball.

Mosquito alighting on my naked thigh:
take your time and suck your fill. I've sworn
never to hurt your kind. You sip my life's juice
but leave my soul intact and never sigh
that I become a mere life-plagued conformist
drear, insignificant, and wound up for malice.

43

for Sid Marty

I am a scratch on a fine print,
a bruising thumbmark.

I have nothing to say to mountains
or their plateaus of air.

Nevertheless they haunt me like remorse;
they hold me by their silence.

Aeons have so perfected it
I can uncover no trace of irony.

Rage alone offers me potence,
rage and avenging hate.

When I fill my soul with them
I am taller than any mountain.

Banff
June 3, 1982

44

Her hair painted henna red
blazed suddenly into fire
and he fell back before her face,
his mouth dry with horror.
Mean-eyed carrion birds
flew from her twisted lips
and the leaping streaks on her head
coiling and uncoiling like snakes
chilled the blood in his veins.
Transfixed by dread
he was freezing into stone
when he remembered how often
her mouth had given him
    the gift of tongue,
how often her beautiful mouth
had praised his poems.

45

It's just as I thought.
                        She has
small eyes, a plain bulbous nose,
and tells me she hasn't had sex in years.
She's also thirty-seven and has short legs.
When I ask her what
she's studying at the university
two nights each week she says: "Theology.
I want to make myself as perfect as the God
I'm getting to know better
                                    seminar
by seminar."

Compassion heaves in my chest
like a vomit
                and I turn away silent.
Of what use are words
when the fates doom a mortal past helping?

46

My friend's mother was proud of her sandpaper hands.

She lifted the chemise
of her young neighbour
and slid them down her breasts.

"See how rough they are," she crowed,
mesmerizing me as she always did
with her two yellow stumps of tooth
and the dark space between.

From the white frigidaire top
Jesus on his plastic crucifix
looked down at us;
beneath his tortured look
the strutting cock was soundless.

The grandfather clock's tick tock
froze in the summer air.

47

for Vivian

The tight sweater she was wearing
showed off her good points at once;
luckily she had an attractive mouth
that lifted my thoughts so that my mind
raced to it from her twin attractions,
settling on neither long enough
to put a glaze on my devouring eyes.

At twenty-one she was explaining for me
why nobody wrote love poems anymore.
"Love's unsatisfied lust, nothing more.
If I want a man I jump into bed with him.
Who needs his heated fantasies, or mine?
I've learned a thing or two about poets:
the only sheets they soil are those they write on.

"If a lover has been fondling my breasts
why should he wish to dream about them
or cudgel his brains to put my nipples into a poem
when he can pop them into his mouth
like ripe berries? I prefer it, mister, that way.
So does he I'm sure, my breasts are so round and firm."
She stopped and I've wondered what old Petrarch would say.

Or lecherous Alighieri who made his Beatrice
immortal by putting his lust into an Inferno.
What if she and Petrarch's Laura had been a good lay
and spoke of their lovers as they might of artichokes,
of ecstasies and fiascos, one-night stands,
finding the comedy of sex too funny for words?
What masterpieces would each have ripped off then?

48

After a volcano erupts
ornaments and charms are shaped
from the boiling lava
propelled down mountainside and slope.

You can buy them
for a song in Sicily or Yucatan
to wear as a talisman
on bared arm or wrist.

So have I made poems
from the black, scalding dross
that poured out
from my raging breast.
Take whatever you wish or can
but don't overlook those
with a harsh, singular beauty
in their carved nakedness.

49

for William Goodwin

Fabrizio is wise. The stars tell him all
he needs to know: that foreplay ends in boredom
or despair, that greed and lust agitate
the treacherous ant heaps till disaster comes
to smash them with the conqueror's thicker heel.
He scans the heavens for sense and there finds none,
nor in his wife's scrawny arms and devotions;
sons can disappoint but see him rally
to advance a nephew's human need for gold,
a fair face; recollection and desire
stirring the embers in his slack loins
till a scholar's self-irony snuffs out
the small flame licking at his groin
to leave him seedy before the noble's choice
'twixt sex and death: knowing the choice is each man's
to the very end though the priests and Father Pirrone
rave and wave their superstitious crucifixes
to scare satyrs back to their forbidden wolds
and the diseased bourgeois deed his estates
to the cretinous son, the spoilt daughters.

Cuba
December 31, 1981

68

50

for Alice Duarte

She's Portuguese: chestnut brown eyes,
full sensuous mouth, a lilting English accent
picked up in London from Oxford tutors;
and disguised as Overseas Representative
from *Pegasus Tours.*
  I tell her after 5 mins conversation,
"Knowing you any longer would give me
a fierce neurosis; I'd be torn
between the itch to hear you speak,
so lovely is the soft lilt of your voice,
and wanting to seal your sweet lips
with kisses maddening as wine or glory.
  When, dear Vision, can I see you
so I can have my promised breakdown?"
To my eternal delight
                              the tall full-bosomed goddess
smiling, responds with a wink,
"Whenever you please, my Lord."

51

for Veneranda

7 A.M. He switches the light on in the kitchen.
Pale yellow. The colour of beaten egg
mixed with milk, sunspots on all the walls.
He picks up a book to read. His woman
still keeps the stars in her head. She dreams.
Of what? Of the perfect existential lover
who will give her no more trouble. Of a love
that walks confident as an animal.
She has suffered so much from love, from men
who are not the right kind of animal. When
she gives herself she demands nothing more
than glasses brimming with red wine, and laughter.
What can she ever do with spilled wine
and broken glasses; with laughter that makes
a place nobody can live in except necrophiles
and warlocks?
     He tiptoes into her bedroom
and leaves three sincere kisses on her pillow.

Montreal
September 16, 1981

52

for Diane Parent

May the gods be praised that I should meet
on my final lap to the eternal sea
one so young, so gracious and lovely,
under clear skies promising as herself.
Ankled deep in the scorching sands
I can hear the shouting tide; in it
invitation and menace like the smile
on the fair face of my companion,
making me wish to nuzzle forever
between her firm thighs and cover
her mouth with long hungering kisses.

Insensate to everything but her warm flesh
I'd float out into the voluptuous sea,
my practised breast stroke perfect at last.
The heaving mounds press against me,
alluring me past the white wavecrests
that close behind like tall portals
barring return. Green towers collapse
on bright medallions larger than suns;
the virginal foam breaks into bridal cries
and after the last loud crash of savaging breasts,
into the long silence that no man hears.

Cuba
December 30, 1981

53

for Lisa

I've seen your singular smile elsewhere.
On sun-warmed Mediterranean statues
of the late Alexandrian period.

With your fragile, ever-smiling lips you appear
both sensual and ascetic, a coin's toss
sending you either way.

The curves of your mouth bracket your secret.
Which are you? Mary, mother of Jesus,
or that other Mary, the scarlet Magdalene.

Your secret is that you don't know.
So you smile often to conceal your confusion,
giving you that strange look that intrigues us all.

Your lips obsess me like a misremembered word.
I can't remove them from my head, or imagine
any greater triumph than to blot them out forever.

At fourteen I made an older girl
articulate "prunes" over and over again
because her mouth shaped beautifully pronouncing it.

Yours, I finally conclude, is the smile of a woman
who, figure and face making her irresistible,
mocks her lovers' immoderate passion.

But mostly mocks the world and herself,

knowing how brief are the days of beauty;
how cruel and fleeting the loves they inspire.

Banff
August 15, 1981

54

For her, sex is something she holds in reserve;
alienated from her real inner self,
it's tended with care like some exotic plant
to allure the stray butterfly to her sill.
She takes Yoga classes and watches what she eats,
is prudent about money and emotions
but unfurls her independence like a flag.
Having been in analysis for insight
(so she informs me) and not therapy
she discusses love as an abstract painting,
a flowing involuted figure by Moore.
She likes catching it out when it makes its spring
and holding its quivering form up to the light,
yet wonders why it blackens and disappears
or grows into some bloated attachment
that mocks her with mouths shaped like grotesque suckers.
An artist in living, she swears by passion
and spontaneity, mistaking fervent
loquacity for something she's too cool,
too cautious to possess, too ungiving
in the modern sense; dismaying the lost men
who circle around her long shapely neck
until they break from the enchantment and run.
It always baffles her she's so much alone
or with old lovers, mostly now with women,
for her mirroring image shows her beautiful
and the great Moore had once praised her talent.
It would be a mercy to make her see
the fault's not entirely hers; it's in the stars,
in the revolving potter's wheel that's sent the sexes
flying off in contrary directions to wander
among sapless words that hang in the air

like stricken November leaves no wind has come
to shake loose. Dry November leaves, my dear,
whose ghostly rattle when a small breeze stirs them
expresses your sad vacancies for the world.

55

Pour souls, running after
freedom, love, and laughter
   but laying down their lives
in the arms of their wives

56

If you were to walk down this foreign street
with its narrow trouser-pants sidewalks
and flics standing on every corner,
sometimes in twos and threes
I could imagine the April sun
rolling like a ball between the tall buildings.

Flags would appear from every window
to wave it on;
they'd break sonorously into the national anthem
of any country I thought about
and the manikins behind their plate glass windows
start laughing for the sheer hell of it.

You'd begin to notice
as you came closer to where I was standing
on my head
that everything was dissolving all around you.
There was no East or West, no North or South;
only my feet waving in the air.

You'd understand then for the first time
what your orifices mean to me;
why their absence brings the sun down from the sky
and my heart begins to flutter like a thousand flags.
Run faster than the sun, my love,
for just one second ago I grimaced like a manikin.

Paris
April 23, 1982

57

for Lisa Ross

Other women I've had in my rooms.
They all attempted seduction by getting me to talk.
When I'm aroused I speak beautifully.
I mistake my love of words for that of the woman
    who inspired them.
This will explain why I married four times.
A point is always reached when I can't distinguish
    between lust and language;
when holding a desired woman in my arms,
    her nipples become the fat pink syllables
I roll on my tongue.

Dear Lisa, after the third glass when my eloquence
was putting the familiar ache in my crotch
only rhetoric can evoke
and I knew that the next dazzling metaphor
    would give me an erection for sure,
luckily (the fates are sometimes kind) I misused a word.
The spell was broken. The pain in my groin faded,
and pulling off the sexual mist I'd robed you in
as if it were blouse or shift, felt I was home safe,
    when cold as an icepick I asked:
"What do you think of Mitterand?"

58

Death cut him down like a tall pine
after letting him hack his lungs out
with TB. I well remember his blue eyes,
his aquiline nose; Roman I'd have said
had I been Miss Thorpe's pupil in Grade Nine
but I was barely eleven when he died
and Caesar not even a name. Pompey neither.
I, at least, had the warrant of age
but my other brothers seemed runts when they
walked beside him so very tall he was
— tall and straight as a woodland pine
but each day growing more peremptory,
more fractious and unlovable as he wasted
under the white blankets my mother bleached
and ironed for him day after day.
                              And so,
after they'd washed his body and robed him
in his cerements he was too long for the coffin
and I watched, horrified, from my safe hole
two voiceless men lean on his knob to push
it down, making the stiffened feet jump up
as though he were a runner preparing
for an Olympic track or a harlequin,
full of inventive tricks, about to appear
for the crowd's applause. Now another pair,
blackbearded and waiting in silence
at the casket's other end, shoved
his feet in (I still hear their
scraping sound against the board)
and I saw his head rise up suddenly
like that of a drowning man surfacing to take
one final look before going down forever.
                              Again
they pressed down on his skull, this time hard,

and the bare rodlike feet flew out
above the planed edge of the bone box ready,
it seemed, to walk on air or to start
running, so forceful had been their thrust
into the fetid, overheated room. It surprised me
to see them halted in mid-air, stiff and white
as if they'd already turned to chalk. It didn't
look right somehow and though damp all over,
a fine chill went down my back and I began
to retch loudly, exposing me all at once
to eyes that flew at me like released wasps.
                                        Now
that I'm far away from that strange hour
I'm more prudent or luckier as to where
I find my metaphors for life and death,
those fragments of lived experience
a man converts into consolatory hints
or the needed culm for self-propulsion
towards the paling stars, or for self-excuse:
yet can't quite empty my imagination
of the ludicrous seesaw that finished only
when they crooked my brother's unoiled knees,
afterwards banging the coffinlid tight
while I prayed for the wordless attendants
to begin their morning devotions,
turning whiter than his cooled corse
before tightlipped with fear I bolted
for the familiar kitchen smells
and the rude affection in my mother's hands.

59

for Malka Cohen, 1897–1981

The last indignities are over:
the bar between convulsing jaws;
gaunt cheeks, death's familiar foxholes,
and breasts that once gave suck,
now flat and unresponsive as damp rags;
her diminutive teats, raw and wornout,
mocking our vaporous presence on earth
with the mordant emphasis of quotemarks.

If ten devils possessed me
I'd flaunt my scorn for this stale farce
that made Lear and Achilles weep
and pluck those shrivelled paps looking
like forgotten berries on winter's snow;
razor the mortician's balls and grow them
like bleeding rose bulbs in the urine bottle
empty and open to the nurse's hand.

Where's my kinswoman with her blue-black hair,
strong white teeth, peasant health,
her high colour and highboned cheeks?
Is this she, now so shrunk and quiet,
the cannula still in her vein
that supplied her seven rebel parts
till the common axeman
dismissed them all with one soundless blow?

Shall I never touch her warm hand again?
Never again look on her fluttering lids
or praise her rough affection for child and friend?
The white walls are mute. And no clever instrument

waits outside in the blank corridors
to graph incoherency and human rage
or the hopeless, homeless love
of her weeping daughters.

60

Everyone laughed when he told the assembly
how the famous rebel poet was captured.

They laughed even louder
when he described for them
with many jokes and asides
the next day's activity.

How they had pulled his ears
away from the skull
and made him chew and swallow them,
first one then the other.

Because they had seasoned
the bleeding ears with Fr. mustard
his compatriots, when they see him,
laughingly cry to one another:
"There goes Moutarde."

The sight of his earless head
cracks everyone up
even at funerals
and solemn commemorative parades.

Everyone says
he's eligible for a pension.

61

You stand dumb and tall, Dante.
Even your famed eagle schnozz
is dripping pigeonshit.

Uncaring of your pain and exile
the teachered schoolchildren
turn barnyard fowls, cackle.

Or hoot like young owls
when the taller boys, snickering loudly,
read the eternal commedias
scratched on your pedestal:

TI AMO ETTORE

FLORA
4–8–81
ESPANOL

Verona
April 10, 1981

62

for Boris Pasternak

The bomb that makes the rubble
leap into the air
                         lifts him up, he says,
"to the seventh heaven."

The fires it starts in the streets
are festivals. Houses reel on their foundations
like joyful drunks
and joining their reveller's hands
throw themselves all together
into the fiery bacchanalia.

All day he has waited patiently
for the enemy planes
                         to fly over the city
and perform their holy work of destruction,
scouring from people's souls
the dictatorship's rust of malice and fear.

His poet's heart flutters with happiness.
Burn, city, burn. Your blazing embers
are seeds for a nobler civilization.

But how will he keep the ecstasy
from showing in his face and trembling hands
when he goes down to the tenants
and lovingly touching their grey faces
tells them POSHAR PATOOSHEN
 – it's all clear, the fire's out?

63

Boris, you were soft as a boiled potato.
No Hemingway, women had you by your balls
all you life though you had the good sense
to stick with two of them to the very end.
  Apartments of your own divided mind,
you craved to have at once passion and order,
adventure and security; the sure bridge
spanning the terrifying chasm below.
Contrary winds turned you like a weathercock.

Was it weakness made you write the gospel poems,
blubbering at the foot of the Cross
where you'd flung yourself–a baptized unheroic Jew;
pen for an antisemitic vodka-swilling boor
  a shifty unforgivable missive
begging him to let you stay in that foul land
where every lout and time-serving scribbler
might fling his dirt at you?
Leer as you wiped the filth from your open face?

Maybe the fault lay in your Jewish genes,
in your terrible need to suffer and to please.
Or was it, after all, only the bored indifference
of transcendent genius that moves always
  on the twin rails of here and beyond, the ideal
and actual, but unerringly to that great good place
where Dr. Zhivago opens its welcoming arms
to seer and sod, revolutionist and pharisee,
and poems stay perfect in the mind of God?

64

What it comes down to, Boris,
is that you're no less a fool
than the rest of us. You love the woman
but you want to be free. You want
to be free but your loins at night
ache and you can't get her face
out of your mind. Your cowardice,
too, is par for the course. Though your life
is hell on earth you won't leave your wife
and go live with the woman you love.
You've got scruples, haven't you? Of course
you have. Build your happiness
on someone else's misery? Not you, Boris.
That would betray the favourite snapshot
you have of yourself, the one you cling to
most ferociously when you're being pulled
from all sides. So you meet clandestinely
in her room to snatch an embrace before
your lover throws another of her tantrums
or the squabbling begins. Since you own
the merciless self-awareness of the poet,
no one knows better than yourself how silly
are the excuses you make while exhibiting
in almost equal proportion tenderness, candour,
and heartlessness, knowing in the end
your innocent charm will get you off the hook
and earn for you her forgiving smile. Why?
Because the lady is young and nuts
about you, even when you flap about
like loose awning in the storm of words
you let fall on her dear head so you won't hear
your own self-contempt gnawing at your vitals;
even when you're a pitiful caricature

of the ideal poet whose image you carry
in your head and betray with each word or deed
and even, as now, with the very silence
in which your next poem is taking form.

65

Slowly they grow towards extinction.
My window has seen the winter's blasts
but looks on as impassively
as city crowds when a man is beaten.

It holds their reflection for me
like a perfect work of art;
on sullen days I'm moved to ecstasy
by images of beauty and death.

The leaves shiver at the rain's touch;
like old men when the weather's bad
they draw in at their own bareness,
huddling to learn its dark promise.

The sun-created trees do not create
but let the winds whip and strip them;
coralling their empery into space
they perform their simple roles and wait.

They wear the same uniforms year to year
and march into the centuries
lashed by sergeants Rain and Snow,
stopping to re-group in oases.

A trillion leaves appear and fall;
season after season they come and go.
I stare out from my sterile window.
Even the trees are without faith.

Blindly they put forth, sicken and die.
I am the sole meaning they have;
only if I will it to happen
will they shoot from their roots and fly.

66

To go with genius
   the whole distance
is to walk straight into Thanatos
with a greeting smile
   to match his own.

Hard to come that near to death;
harder still
   not to frown.

67

Orgulous man dancing
on your platform of misdeeds and folly,
look at the crumpled leaves
huddled against my garage door.

Visit with me
the close-by cemeteries
whose blank script you alone can fill
with what you remember as alive and human.

Dancing man, you are no more
than the wind that propels
you undissuably towards
the waiting grave.

You lift
a bright or dull shingle,
fill a sail, and after there remain
only your songs and poems and laughter.

Niagara-on-the-Lake
September 4, 1981

68

Louis, what the hell!
Let's bury the hatchet
(and this time not
in each other's neck or skull).
 We're both grey around the edges
and facing ills that age brings:
arthritis, heaviness of gait,
loss of teeth and sight; the
weariness that sets in at the close
 when life's seen as puppet show,
the colours fading from the stock figures;
and hate's fury or ambition's
sounding like tapes reeled backwards.

We've gone our separate ways
to Valhalla – so what?
 We still keep our rage
for bourgeois and huckster,
still scorn the fashionable lies
of pulpit and marketplace;
still keep faith with Homer and Shakespeare,
John Donne and Yeats.
 In that clamorous brotherhood
bound together by ties
mightier than nation or blood
we invoke in the gathering dusk
the dear death-cheating names
of Glassco and Smith and Klein.

My left ear partly deaf,
I only half-heard your diatribes
 and literary abuse,
the gossip seething in the streets

that malice grows from grin to crooked grin.
I hope, Louis, you were similarly afflicted
   and only half-heard mine.
As for old fishwives' tales
I know your famed humanity
stopped up your ears
till they fell to earth like tattered kites.
   Dear friend, dear comrade-in-arms,
in the darker nights ahead
which the revolving sun
relentlessly spins for both of us
   let us forgive utterly
the long, divisive years, the pain
and may each in his separate sky
with undiminished fire, shine.

69

I'd like my soul to have the same leathery skin
as this zucchini I found in an abandoned basin;
wind and frost have hardened it. I can tell
not even the hottest water will make it edible.

It's spare and curved like an old woman;
long ago it gave up trying to please,
and lies in the moist palm of my hand indifferent
to the amused and pitying look in my eyes.

It accepts its difference without a whimper
or recourse to the big words that pass for wisdom,
especially if they're rhymed or written vertically.
Tough, she's ready for the big blasts. Let them come.

Were I a small child again I'd deck it in hat and shawl
and if its firm spirit didn't terrify me
I'd give it small lustrous eyes
and gouge out a mouth, greying and small.

There, look now: it has dignity with decrepitude.
It's almost as if I held my shrunken mother
in my hands. Nothing could ever content her. Like her
my zucchini spits on the world and is rude.

I'm too fearful to turn my head away.
Only the incantation of some powerful verse
can withdraw me from its demonic sway.
In my entranced ears takes shape a familiar curse.

From poets too I'd like to have direct speech,
no snivelling, each word like a blow.
In rainless deserts the cacti open to the sun
and their perfume is the other language buzzards know.

70

Paraplegics
on a volleyball court
batting the poem across the net
with steel fingers.

Between games, earnestly
debating the newest
Olympian records
for pole-vaulting and track.

Or writing reviews
for *Maclean's* and *The Fiddlehead*,
scratching them on sand
with the thick end of their crutches.

One loves them dearly
and drops endless
tears, silent and bitter,
into the long dark nights.

71

Furtively
with many sudden stops
the squirrel outside my window
advances on tree and can.

The creature wants his breakfast.

He never looks at me
to whine:
"What's a Canadian?"

He never yaps:
"The world's a hospital
and we're all sick.
Lower your voice, Layton."

He never intones:
"I'm a sinful haired rat
who must keep clean
and please everyone."
No one has heard him pray for sunshine
or more nuts.

Dear Bushytail,
I know you're hungry
and have many fears
but a pert gallantry
shows in every leap you make.

Now stop a moment and tell me,
"Whatcha doin' in this country?"

72

She dances like a solitary bacchante

The tight miniskirt she flicks
before my eyes
is a leopard's ever-changing
spots

On the crowded dancefloor
she dances like someone possessed
and I am lost to all
except the motion
of her disordering limbs

When she dances like that
I can follow her down
all the way down
into the smoky bowels of hell

73

The nerved-up lines jerkily
trying to keep pace
with the horror
                to outfox it
perhaps even outrun it
for the Governor General's medal

Whatever the notations of pain:
the crab's severed claw,
the penknife beside the woman's
bleeding cunt,
the putrefying snake
                    its sweet stink
in the summer dry grass
. . . to appear always cool,
never raising the voice
in anger or revulsion
. . . the perfect drawing-room voice
for Canada's gentility

Life's gross indecencies
of killing & fucking
vised expertly in lines
to fall like icicles
on eyes & tongue

But the sacral odour
is ineffaceable
and finally suffocates

Alas, poor Yorick,
there's vanity even in that;
in going down for the last time,

a soulful look in your eyes
for the photographers

Even the self-disgust
is a kind of pleasure
                    obscene
you keep telling yourself
because you're civilized
and thrill to Mozart & Saint Joan

74

I was mistaken:
poetry's not an Eden of pleasures,
it's a minefield of linguistic problems.

Magic? Ah, no;
it's categories laced with themes.
Not the colourful agitation
of a butterfly
but the ugly caterpillar
trailing its excrement
on a green leaf.

I believed poetry
was the ecstasy of murder or sex.
Plainly I was wrong;
it's the constipated ruminations
of castratos and pacifists.

75

for Giorgio Morandi

In Bologna
I learned of an artist
who'd painted only bottles.
The ristorantes must have been
crowded and noisy
as they are now
and the expensive shops
filled with priceless things
only money can buy
but he painted only bottles.
He must have seen
the ancient churches and squares,
the famous university and monuments;
he must have eaten
prosciutto, salamis, tortellini
and drunk the sparkling wines
of Bologna:
he painted only bottles.
Mussolini came and went,
likewise the war,
Hiroshima, the Holocaust,
Stalin, the smooth displacement of culture
by pornography:
he painted only bottles
and one famous self-portrait.
There must be a deep meaning
in this somewhere
but what it is
I cannot tell
but must wait for instruction
from a wise old whore
a philosopher
or death at my door.

76

Beautiful, wearing a silver crucifix,
Rosa works in the waterfront bar
as a call girl who does not answer.

All the girls jump from their stools
when the Neapolitans point at them
— but not Rosa.

When the young Mafioso
orders her up to bring his rum and Coke
she offers him the tribute of a slow smile
and takes her time.

Sensing he's different from the others
and knows his worth,
knows he has the sharpest knife
in the city
and two Alsatians that love him.

Naples
April 15, 1982

77

for Patrick Crean

Odd, that like myself you've been married
four times;
and yet I could have foretold your story
at our first greeting.

You're much too good-looking for clamorous women
to leave alone
and your subtle intelligence is no defence
against their resolution.

Your vanity needs their nurturing attention
and flattery;
too soon you discovered the immense world of commonness:
their loves singled you out.

You have the hedonist's scorn for strife and busyness,
the moiling masses;
believing a sensible man will find all of life's charms
in a champagne glass.

Anyway, that it's a fine talisman against the emptiness
that comes as much with success
these days as with failure, leaving you ever-hungering
for a woman's kisses.

At the end what's the litany? Betrayals:
loves, hopes for the human race,
the traitorous face, the incontinent bladder.
The press of flesh on flesh staves off surrender.

For we're romantics, you and I; in our century near kin

to the sick christian
in a christless world whose bleak terrors we choose to inter
between a woman's thighs.

78

A milkwhite kitten
curled up
   on the bough
of an appletree

A gigantic blossom
until
      its green eyes
blink

79

for Simon Stone

The snake in his hands
rigid
      glistens
fills the place with imprecations
a subterranean anguish
                            a flash
of pain
        terrene
with abrupt cries
that break from the lips
of a pagan god
              sundering
chains from wrists and ankles
his passion
direct as a sudden blow as
a sudden unexpected kiss

Biddle's
October 15, 1982

80

"The trouble with time," the old man cried,
"it's linear and long drawn-out,
a spool of black thread.
I must wait impossible ages
before the red Mafia in the Kremlin
croaks;
as long as half-a-century
before the motorized Mongols
at Poland's gates
are once again sweet-smelling dust.

"In time it happens
after the spilling of much blood
an Attila or Stalin
is strangled by that black thread.

"But time rounded as a cusp, oval,
allows me to imagine an instant
bursting open like a bomb
and reducing everything ugly and menacing
to the nothing
it's on the way to becoming."

Verona
April 10, 1981

81

A fenced-in swimming pool,
American style with potted shrubs,
trimmed hedges

At the neighbouring tables
some Nipponese, polite, always smiling

Nobody hearing me, I splinter
the wide plateglass window,
flinging my boyhood heart
into the pool

I watch it sink
to the pool's bottom like a polyp
where it will lie buried
under the long re-forming scintillations

When I look up
the children of the celestial bear
have stopped smiling
over the hardboiled eggs, the white toast

Tokyo
October 26, 1981

82

It's nice to be with young bearded Italians,
idealistic Marxists up to their wet ears
in the politics of vision

They make me forget greying hairs
and the flatulency and cynicism
they bring with them

Against my superior judgment
I find myself listening.
What if their glorious Future is remote

As the sun? As the sun it warms.
Their happy babble cheers me
like barnyard noises in spring

Just attend to that loud rooster
crowing over his vanquished enemies.
What crushing eloquence! What vitality!

My disdain is thinned by envy.
I shall not pass this way again.
One does not dream with eyes open

Yet even as I sink into their pleasant stupor
I count the skulls under their marching feet
and wonder what cages they have readied

For the Pasternaks whom power dismays.
The eternal dialetic of sex and death
does not interest them. Nor the beauty

I behold in the darkening sky.
For now they drink the boisterous wine,

their mouths full of words and spiced bologna

Their smiles genuine as the region's cheese.
Happy, happy fools. O to be young and flaunt
one's generous sentiments all night long!

Fiano
April 14, 1981

83

Demented apes
who comb
their hair

Every day
humans grow
more entrancingly evil

Tomorrow or next year,
smiling politely
and showing their polished teeth

They'll devour
each other's kidneys
for their evening meal

Discussing Relativity
Amnesty International
Kafka's Hunger Artist

84

The dog runs past,
taking my thoughts of Infinity with him;
at the corner
he's swallowed up in it
and when he clambers back
I observe he has three heads
and his coat is scorched.

Not one of the nobs
will tell me where it's been
or what Greek it encountered
or the name of its dentist.
I light my cigar
at their singular redhot tail.

It's pointless to explore
the subject of Love with them
or Beauty or Man's Fate
on this planet.
Philosophy and Art
only make them growl;
in their collective minds
everything is cut and dried
and fixed forever
and there is only Hell.

But why does my head spin
at the sight of a beautiful woman
and the swirl of her skirt
pleasure me with hurt?
And why am I,
who find a leaf mysterious
and a spear of grass
or the bark of a dog

or croak of a frog
confident as if I'd been told
that not Hell, O not Hell,
but Love alone provides
the central heating for the world?

85

He wants to burn
all the encyclopedias
in his library.

Only once when he smoked dope
did they come out of their shelves
to do a hopak.
Then it was the minuet.
Finally, a waltz.

Never before
had they given him so much pleasure.

Dionysians for a night
they answered all his questions
except one:
what is it about ignorance
that makes its possessor
appear so strong?

86

They've never had a good press;
only those with their mother's milk
still on their lips
trust them

"Leeches" "Lice"
"Bats and Succubi let loose
from blackest hell"
are poets' names for them

In unadorned fact
they're poor bastards
looking for a buck

Are minions of the rich,
paid to tighten the blindfold
on the eyes of Justice

Are hardnosed chippies
whose words are for hire
to the highest bidder

Are trained liars
with a licence
to serve their countrymen

And are as indispensable
to the well-ordered state
as its undertakers & trashmen

87

Trained in the best schools
of the realm
to kill without pity or sorrow

He nevertheless spared an old Jew
who resembled a beloved teacher
in the Hochschule

Not able to still the sharp needles
of conscience
he drank to blot out his shame and guilt

Expelled from the Partei
for a weak-willed bullying drunk
our brave Klaus shot himself finally

88

Comrade Undershaftsky's a poet;
also First Deputy Minister of Culture
in a land where there isn't any,
the real poets and novelists
having been silenced
one way or another.

But you won't hear him saying that
as he turns his well-fed gaze
on you,
a brochure in each eye,
to proclaim from the security
of his large office
that he doesn't want anyone
to find his skull
without a hole
from bullet or knife.

In Bulgaria
they've abolished
not only capitalists and landlords
but also
bad taste.

Finally out of patience
with him,
I insert a poem
by Mandelstam
between the pages
of his book
and watch it go up
in flame and smoke,

the poem remaining
mysteriously intact,
not even singed
at the edges.

89

I visited many lands.
Korea, the most remote
boasts thirty-five monuments
honouring its dead poets.

Canada
was the only country
where I experienced culture shock.

90

for Joe Kertes

When they weren't killing off Indians
for their furs and territory,
or corrupting senators and councilmen,
or making money off brains more inventive
than their own, the Canadian bourgeois
filtered their piety and wealth
into endowments for church choirs, libraries,
and hospitals; sure of the place they deserved
on this sinful earth and of the golden
Edwardian chair waiting for them in heaven.

Conventional as his sets of Dickens and Maryat,
Calvin McQuesten, honourable founder of a line,
esteemed doctor and foundryman,
married three times, his third wife
running through his fortune like a devouring
plague, squandering it on clothes,
bric-a-brac, and expensive china. Among
his descendants can be counted two lawyers, one
alderman, one minister, one probable suicide;
and Ruby McQuesten 1878–1911
who painted excellent watercolours, never married,
and died of tuberculosis. Of her numerous clan,
she alone learned the art of living
and lived each day joyously, a freak
like Galsworthy's Bosinney and quite unlike
her siblings and forbears who met,
after their Presbyterian immersions
in the church font next door,
human wretchedness as best they could
with solid acquisitions and visible good works.

Hamilton, Ont.,
July 12, 1983

91

for Annette Pottier

At my invitation
she comes to see me.
She is young and gorgeous.

And I am seventy
plagued by memories
and arthritis.

Let Lear and Oedipus rant
on all the stages of the world.
They were but blind old men.

92

His old fingers making wet
the hairy monster under her lace tunic,
he hears the deft-handed goddess
tell across the torn coverlet
how once, still a copper-haired *kori*
in Piraeus,
she watched her grandfather
slit the pig's throat
ear to ear;
afterwards hearing
the hot blood of the crazed animal,
dying on his four trotters,
spurt into the white enamel pot;
all the while thinking
of the small fast thunders
the first gouts of rain
made on her roof,
the wind howling all night long:
a decrepit satyr lost
briar-trapped in a dark, dank grove
and in pain.

93

The train chuffs its way to the station
   roaring like an old bull in pain.
Close your eyes, a god is being slain.

At the platform's wooden edge
   the vegetation is slowly dying;
stricken are bramble, grass, and sedge.

In varying hues of orange and yellow
   the October leaves are giving up the ghost
and lie on the ground, forsaken, lost.

Intent as remorse or intolerable guilt
   a small wind turns up my collar.
The earth, everywhere I look, is a covered bier.

Distantly, a flaming maple mocks the season:
   an old man obsessively imagining
a young girl's limbs, her passion-moist nest.

94

Where is he? Tall and muscular,
he went into the ring
to beat the brains out of his opponent;
afterwards when he leaned over me
like the tower of Pisa
his grey eyes laughed.

Why after half a century
won't his image leave me? Does
repressed envy lie dormant like a seed
to ripen again and again
like immortelles?

Is he still living?
Did he have a good life? Father sturdy children?
Make some woman happy
despite the odds against that happening?
Or did he end up
a used-up executive in Niagara-on-the-Lake,
obese and disgruntled?

Perhaps he's at the golf links
where I'll find him swinging a club.
If I recognize him
what shall I say?

Why does his imagined face
so move me
after all these years?

Niagara-on-the-Lake
September 15, 1982

95

When she climbs the steps of her basement apartment
she leaves the place in absolute darkness
except for the small mirror in my mind
that holds her surprised reflection.

I polish it till her confident smile
lights up my eyes and when I whisper
in the dark: "I love you with all my heart,"
the corners of the room begin to shine.

She will bring wine and two goblets
and we'll toast my familiar daimons,
my obsession with her mad-making limbs:
cry window-breaking huzzas for her vagrant soul.

I've flicked off the years, one by one:
"This one loved me, this one didn't."
Tonight I'll give her the denuded stalk
and it will turn a sunflower in her hand.

Roxboro
December 31, 1982

96

for Doug Beardsley

I'd like to write a poem
as taut and thrilling
as my pain,
with sharp zigzags into laughter
at the comedy of it all.

Ha, Ha! Pow! Ha, Ha! Pow!
Pow! Pow! Pow! Ha, Ha! Got you!

Ever see a lizard
wipe a dragonfly clean off a wall?
Or a blue heron gargle fish
in her throat?
If you've seen these
you've seen it all.

If that doesn't convince
you might consider the sun
loosening the ribs of a dead mouse
on a perfect day in June.

Serious? Who, me?
You've dialled the wrong number.
Try someone else. I've had four mares
shot from under me
and I'm still riding hard for glory,
but this time
on no other horse than Pegasus.

Niagara-on-the-Lake
August 24, 1981

97

Like a sponge the poet soaks up the sewage
of evil trespass and self-delusion
running through the ruts of this dark epoch.
His head is a black cloud about to burst.

From his own self must come light and truth,
the long-awaited word to stifle discord;
let it be plain as cut parsnip on a plate
or the wall of his house when sunlight strikes.

Utterance alone can heal the ailing spirit
and make man and poet a single self;
bring back on the long vein of memory
the laughter and wholeness of childhood.

Never will he beg off from his pursuit
as did Isaiah though he sees too plain
how impurity and self-betrayal
make the prophet's voice clunk like a cracked bell.

In the creative word lies redemption.
At the darkest hour somewhere the sun,
the life-giving sun, turns feculent swamps
into grasslands where gazelles run and play.

Let it burn out the eyes of his sockets.
He'll stare it down into the terrorized cities;
bring his human fears to it as to a bonfire
and hear his voice chime like a carillon.

98

I take my Anna everywhere.
She is so beautiful she can break
a man's heart with a look,
the proud thrust of her shoulder.

She tells me she will die young.
I tell her all beautiful women have the same
premonition. Brevity is the stamp
of beauty, sealing it in the mouths of men.

I take my Anna everywhere.
She has the unpitying gaze of a goddess.
All the men who see her
want to live their wrecked lives forever.

99

for Sarah

Will you be as beautiful
    as I imagine you?
As sensitive and tender?
    Unloyal or true?
Will you have a sense of wonder
or will you be a pious clod
    imploring an ignorant god?

Few women delight for long.
    Most disappoint.
A sly malcontent
    lies wound up in each.
As I hope to live
a thousand years for my sins
    their poor souls are costive.

When I was young
    I adored every girl
that stopped my breath.
    I lived only for their smiles.
But hopes run with the years
and love brings to this life
    dissension and strife.

At this hour, only a name,
    still unseen, unknown,
time is weaving you
    on his loom of possibility.
When you emerge at 9 P.M.
fully shaped from his frame
    how will you greet me?

Who will you be?

100

Your warty lads are too shy to tell you
they burn to cover your body full length.

But I, a white-haired lecher and famous,
boldly apprise the world I do.

Dear maid, which will pleasure you most:
a young man's shyness or an old man's lust?

IOI

When the senile poet
    half blind half deaf
rose tremblingly on his feet
    to greet me
I blurted out
        "Your lines, sir,
stand up much better
than you do."

Gratified vanity
    making the famed amorist
grin from ear to ear,
his uninterred skull
    became a lump
in my throat.

102

On the cluttered kitchen table
she has left for his morning meal
the fragrance he loves

She has also left
three half-slices of dark toast,
some cheese with knife bladed like a dagger,
handle black and made from rubber;
the ebony contours of coffee making

Piggy that didn't go to market,
the honey's plastic container
sits like a porcine Buddha
poised between smugness and serenity;
the light-brown viscous honey
fills shaped mouth and snout

The confined sweetness the light outlines
barely touches the earlobes;
bland are the eyes, unclouded,
that fix on him their forceless stare

103

Insects display their different shapes
on sunglasses, on table and book;
not one that isn't the slime of time
or doesn't ask from me a wise look.

The butterfly's flutter on a tall stalk
is my heart's beat in space, O gentle
and steady as my best morning thoughts.
I'd paint them or birds were I Chagall.

Give them yarmulkas to fly to
and sobbing music from the shtetl;
they would flap their crazy wings with joy
and make their certain way to Zion.

How easily, it seems, I might dissolve
into my chair or surrounding air;
become the dirt my feet walk upon,
grow bright flowerets instead of hands.

No more than a dog's bark are we all;
leaf fall or cat's momentary fright
on the retina; here, only to
disappear into the endless night.

The grass is waiting to cover me
like a warm overcoat, green with age;
the bough's luxuriant leaves are sleeves
ready to embrace or hold me down.

Nature conspires with and against
me, brief shuttle between womb and tomb;
a centimetre on which is notched
immense vistas of anguish and gloom.

Confidently I sit here and write
though dark shadows gather near the house
and the birds have left off their singing.
The fly's cry is trapped in the neat web.

One day, my head full of summer noise
or an étude by Frédéric Chopin,
the wind lifting me up by the elbows
will hustle me out of the garden.

Other insects shall come, other leaves grow.
This garden will never be empty;
my wraith will be that white butterfly.
Return a thousand years from now and see.

Niagara-on-the-Lake
July 18, 1981

104

for Kim Yang Shik

So many moons ago
by other mountains and tides
you read some poems of mine

Now I've come all the way
from the far side of the world
to embrace you

Imagination with an eyeblink
wipes out space and time
but manifests that narrow place

Where love still grows
like the first violet of spring
with its shy prevailing glow

Seoul
October 26, 1981

105

He who to himself a grief does bind
Learns to dispraise all mankind
But he who speeds the grief as it flies
Keeps a candid love in his eyes.

LIST OF TITLES

ACKNOWLEDGMENTS

For permission to reprint a number of poems in this collection thanks are owing to the editors of the following publications: *Canadian Literature; Canadian Forum; Origins; Waves; Athanor; Exile; Poetry Review; Matrix; Pottersfield Press; Viewpoint; The Canadian Literary Review;* and *The Lunatic Gazette.* Some of these poems appeared in a limited edition of *The Gucci Bag,* published by Mosaic Press.

A Canada Council grant enabled me to compose free from all delaying harassments and to obtain in adequate measure social intercourse, solitude, and sunshine–for me, the three essential esses of creativity.

Printed in Canada